P9-DJU-554

A Collection of
COMFORT &
ENCOURAGEMENT

Today's Classics

Helen Steiner Rice

A Collection of
COMFORT &
ENCOURAGEMENT

BARBOUR
PUBLISHING

A HELEN STEINER RICE ® Product

A Collection of Comfort and Encouragement © 2014 by
Barbour Publishing, Inc.

All poems © Helen Steiner Rice Foundation Fund, LLC,
a wholly owned subsidiary of Cincinnati Museum Center.
All rights reserved.

Published under license from the Helen Steiner Rice
Foundation Fund, LLC.

Print ISBN 978-1-62836-643-3

eBook Editions:
Adobe Digital Edition (.epub) 978-1-63058-075-9
Kindle and MobiPocket Edition (.prc) 978-1-63058-076-6

All rights reserved. No part of this publication may be
reproduced or transmitted for commercial purposes, except
for brief quotations in printed reviews, without written
permission of the publisher.

Published by Barbour Publishing, Inc., P.O. Box 719,
Uhrichsville, Ohio 44683, www.barbourbooks.com

*Our mission is to publish and distribute inspirational products
offering exceptional value and biblical encouragement to the
masses.*

ecpa Member of the
Evangelical Christian
Publishers Association

Printed in the United States of America.

CONTENTS

EVERYDAY
ENCOURAGEMENT

A SURE WAY TO A HAPPY DAY

Happiness is something
  we create in our minds;
It's not something you search for
  and so seldom find.
It's just waking up and beginning the day
By counting our blessings
  and kneeling to pray.
It's giving up thoughts that breed discontent
And accepting what comes
  as a gift heaven sent.
It's giving up wishing for things we have not
And making the best of whatever we've got.
It's knowing that life is determined for us
And pursuing our tasks
  without fret, fume, or fuss. . .
For it's by completing what God gives us to do
That we find real contentment
  and happiness, too.

A WORD OF UNDERSTANDING

May peace and understanding
Give you strength and courage, too,
And may the hours and days ahead
Hold a new hope for you;
For the sorrow that is yours today
Will pass away; and then
You'll find the sun of happiness
Will shine for you again.

MAKE YOUR DAY BRIGHT
BY THINKING RIGHT

Don't start your day by supposin'
   that trouble is just ahead;
It's better to stop supposin'
   and start with a prayer instead...
For supposin' the worst things will happen
   only helps to make them come true,
And you darken the bright, happy moments
   that the dear lord has given to you...
So if you desire to be happy
   and get rid of the misery of dread,
Just give up supposin' the worst things
   and look for the best things instead.

GOD'S STAIRWAY

Step by step we climb day by day
Closer to God with each prayer we pray,
For the cry of the heart offered in prayer
Becomes just another spiritual stair
In the heavenly place where we live anew. . .
So never give up, for it's worth the climb
To live forever in endless time
Where the soul of man is safe and free
To live and love through eternity.

CLIMB TILL YOUR
DREAM COMES TRUE

Often your tasks will be many,
   and more than you think you can do.
Often the road will be rugged,
   and the hills insurmountable, too.
But always remember, the hills ahead
   are never as steep as they seem,
And with faith in your heart, start upward
   and climb till you reach your dream.
For faith is a mover of mountains—
   there's nothing that God cannot do—
So start out today with faith in your heart
   and climb till your dream comes true.

BE GLAD

Be glad that your life has been
  full and complete,
Be glad that you've tasted
  the bitter and sweet.
Be glad that you've walked
  in sunshine and rain,
Be glad that you've felt
  both pleasure and pain.
Be glad that you've had
  such a full, happy life,
Be glad for your joy as well
  as your strife.
Be glad that you've walked
  with courage each day,
Be glad you've had strength
  for each step of the way.
Be glad for the comfort
  that you've found in prayer.
Be glad for God's blessings,
  His love, and His care.

YESTERDAY, TODAY, AND TOMORROW

❦

Yesterday's dead, tomorrow's unborn,
So there's nothing to fear
  and nothing to mourn,
For all that is past and all that has been
Can never return to be lived once again. . .
And what lies ahead or the things that will be
Are still in God's hands, so it is not up to me
To live in the future
  that is God's great unknown,
For the past and the present
  God claims for His own. . .
So all I need do is to live for today
And trust God to show me
  the truth and the way.
For all I need live for is this one little minute,
For life's here and now and eternity's in it.

MOVER OF MOUNTAINS

Faith is a force that is greater
Than knowledge or power or skill,
And the darkest defeat turns to triumph
If you trust in God's wisdom and will,
For faith is a mover of mountains—
There's nothing man cannot achieve
If he has the courage to try it
And then has the faith to believe.

RENEWAL

When life has lost its luster
and it's filled with dull routine,
When you long to run away from it,
seeking pastures new and green,
Remember, no one runs away from life
without finding when they do
That you can't escape the thoughts you think
that are pressing down on you—
So when your heart is heavy
and your day is dull with care,
Instead of trying to escape,
why not withdraw in prayer?
For in prayer there is renewal
of the spirit, mind, and heart,
For everything is lifted up
in which God has a part...
Somehow the good Lord gives us
the power to understand
That He who holds tomorrow
is the One who holds our hands.

SHOWERS OF BLESSINGS

Each day there are showers of blessings
  sent from the Father above,
For God is a great, lavish giver,
  and there is no end to His love. . .
And His grace is more than sufficient,
  His mercy is boundless and deep,
And His infinite blessings are countless,
  and all this we're given to keep
If we but seek God and find Him
  and ask for a bounteous measure
Of this wholly immeasurable offering
  from God's inexhaustible treasure. . .
For no matter how big man's dreams are,
  God's blessings are infinitely more,
For always God's giving is greater
  than what man is asking for.

GOD WILL NOT FAIL YOU

When life seems empty
   and there's no place to go,
When your heart is troubled
   and your spirits are low,
When friends seem few and nobody cares,
There is always God to hear your prayers...
And whatever you're facing
   will seem much less
When you go to God and confide and confess,
For the burden that seems too heavy to bear
God lifts away on the wings of prayer...
And seen through God's eyes
   earthly troubles diminish,
And we're given new strength
   to face and to finish
Life's daily tasks as they come along
If we pray for strength to keep us strong...
So go to our Father when troubles assail you,
For His grace is sufficient
   and He'll never fail you.

GIVE LAVISHLY!
LIVE ABUNDANTLY!

❧

The more you give, the more you get.
The more you laugh, the less you fret.
The more you do unselfishly,
The more you live abundantly.
The more of everything you share,
The more you'll always have to spare.
The more you love, the more you'll find
That life is good and friends are kind,
For only what we give away
Enriches us from day to day.

HELP US TO SEE AND UNDERSTAND

God, give us wider vision to see and understand
That both the sunshine and the showers
   are gifts from Thy great hand,
And teach us that it takes the showers
   to make the flowers grow,
And only in the storms of life
   when the winds of trouble blow
Can man, too, reach maturity
   and grow in faith and grace
And gain the strength and courage
   to enable him to face
Sunny days as well as rain,
   high peaks as well as low,
Knowing that the April showers
   will make May flowers grow. . .
And then at last may we accept
   the sunshine and the showers,
Confident it takes them both
   to make salvation ours.

COMFORT IN
HIS LOVE

GOD LOVES US

We are all God's children
  and He loves us, every one.
He freely and completely forgives
  all that we have done,
Asking only if we're ready
  to follow where He leads,
Content that in His wisdom
  He will answer all our needs.

A PATTERN FOR LIVING

"Love one another as I have loved you"
May seem impossible to do,
But if you will try to trust and believe,
Great are the joys that you will receive.
For love makes us patient,
    understanding, and kind,
And we judge with our hearts
    and not with our minds,
For love works in ways
    that are wondrous and strange,
And there is nothing in life
    that love cannot change,
And all that God promised
    will someday come true
When you love one another
    the way He loved you.

WINGS OF LOVE

The priceless gift of life is love,
For with the help of God above
Love can change the human race
And make this world a better place...
For love dissolves all hate and fear
And makes our vision bright and clear
So we can see and rise above
Our pettiness on wings of love

GOD'S LOVE

God's love is like an island
   in life's ocean vast and wide—
A peaceful, quiet shelter
   from the restless, rising tide.
God's love is like an anchor
   when the angry billows roll—
A mooring in the storms of life,
   a stronghold for the soul.
God's love is like a fortress,
   and we seek protection there
When the waves of tribulation
   seem to drown us in despair.
God's love is like a harbor
   where our souls can find sweet rest
From the struggle and the tension
   of life's fast and futile quest.
God's love is like a beacon
   burning bright with faith and prayer,
And through the changing scenes of life,
   we can find a haven there.

GOD IS NEVER BEYOND
OUR REACH

No one ever sought the Father
  and found He was not there,
And no burden is too heavy
  to be lightened by a prayer.
No problem is too intricate,
  and no sorrow that we face
Is too deep and devastating
  to be softened by His grace.
No trials and tribulations
  are beyond what we can bear
If we share them with our Father
  as we talk to Him in prayer. . .
We are His erring children
  and He loves us, every one,
And He freely and completely
  forgives all that we have done,
Asking only if we're ready
  to follow where He leads,
Content that in His wisdom
  He will answer all our needs.

GOD'S KEEPING

To be in God's keeping is surely a blessing,
For though life is often dark and distressing,
No day is too dark and no burden too great
That God in His love cannot penetrate.

DO NOT BE ANXIOUS

Do not be anxious, said our Lord,
Have peace from day to day—
The lilies neither toil nor spin,
Yet none are clothed as they.
The meadowlark with sweetest song
Fears not for bread or nest
Because he trusts our Father's love
And God knows what is best.

HE LOVES YOU

It's amazing and incredible
But it's as true as it can be—
God loves and understands us all,
And that means you and me.
His grace is all-sufficient
For both the young and old,
For the lonely and the timid,
For the brash and for the bold.
His love knows no exceptions,
So never feel excluded,
No matter who or what you are,
Your name has been included. . .
And no matter what your problem is,
Just place it in His hand. . .
For in all our unloveliness
This Great God loves us still—
He loved us since the world began,
And what's more, He always will!

LOVE DIVINE, ALL LOVES EXCELLING

❧

In a myriad of miraculous ways
God shapes our lives and changes our days.
Beyond our will or even knowing
God keeps our spirits ever growing.
For lights and shadows, sun and rain,
Sadness and gladness, joy and pain
Combine to make our lives complete
And give us victory through defeat.
Oh "Love divine, all loves excelling,"
In troubled hearts You just keep on dwelling,
Patiently waiting for a prodigal son
To say at last, "Thy will be done."

ENFOLDED IN HIS LOVE

The love of God surrounds us
Like the air we breathe around us,
As near as a heartbeat, as close as a prayer,
And whenever we need Him,
  He'll always be there!

SOMEBODY LOVES YOU

Somebody loves you more than you know,
Somebody goes with you wherever you go,
Somebody really and truly cares
And lovingly listens to all of your prayers. . .
Don't doubt for a minute that this is not true,
For God loves His children
 and takes care of them, too. . .
And all of His treasures are yours to share
If you love Him completely
 and show that you care. . .
And if you walk in His footsteps
 and have faith to believe,
There's nothing you ask for
 that you will not receive!

NEVER BE DISCOURAGED

There is really nothing we need know
  or even try to understand
If we refuse to be discouraged
  and trust God's guiding hand,
So take heart and meet each minute
  with faith in God's great love,
Aware that every day of life
  is controlled by God above.
And never dread tomorrow
  or what the future brings.
Just pray for strength and courage
  and trust God in all things,
And never grow discouraged—
  be patient and just wait,
For God never comes too early,
  and He never comes too late.

ON THE WINGS OF PRAYER

On the wings of prayer
  our burdens take flight
And our load of care becomes bearably light
And our heavy hearts are lifted above
To be healed by the balm
  of God's wonderful love...
And the tears in our eyes
  are dried by the hands
Of a loving Father who understands
All of our problems, our fears and despair,
When we take them to Him
  on the wings of prayer.

THE
ENCOURAGEMENT
OF FRIENDS

WHERE THERE IS LOVE

Where there is love the heart is light;
Where there is love the day is bright.
Where there is love there is a song
To help when things are going wrong.
Where there is love there is a smile
To make all things seem more worthwhile.
Where there is love there's a quiet peace,
A tranquil place where turmoils cease.
Love changes darkness into light
And makes the heart take wingless flight.
Oh, blessed are those who walk in love;
They also walk with God above.

THE GIFT OF FRIENDSHIP

Friendship is a priceless gift
    that cannot be bought or sold,
But its value is far greater
    than a mountain made of gold—
For gold is cold and lifeless,
    it can neither see nor hear,
And in the time of trouble
    it is powerless to cheer.
It has no ears to listen,
    no heart to understand;
It cannot bring you comfort
    or reach out a helping hand—
So when you ask God for a gift,
    be thankful if He sends
Not diamonds, pearls, or riches,
    but the love of real, true friends.

A FRIEND IS A GIFT FROM GOD

Among the great and glorious gifts
   our heavenly Father sends
Is the gift of understanding
   that we find in loving friends.
For somehow in the generous heart
   of loving, faithful friends,
The good God, in His charity
   and wisdom, always sends
A sense of understanding
   and the power of perception
And mixes these fine qualities
   with kindness and affection.
We seek a true and trusted friend
   in the knowledge that we'll find
A heart that's sympathetic
   and an understanding mind.
And often just without a word
   there seems to be a union
Of thoughts and kindred feelings,
   for God gives true friends communion.

DISCOURAGEMENT AND DREAMS

So many things in the line of duty
Drain us of effort and leave us no beauty,
And the dust of the soul
   grows thick and unswept;
The spirit is drenched in tears unwept.
But just as we fall beside the road,
Discouraged with life
   and bowed down with our load,
We lift our eyes, and what seemed a dead end
Is the street of dreams
   where we meet a friend.

UNEXPECTED ANGELS

The unexpected kindness
  from an unexpected place,
A hand outstretched in friendship,
  a smile on someone's face,
A word of understanding
  spoken in a time of trial
Are unexpected miracles
  that make life more worthwhile.
For God has many messengers
  we fail to recognize,
But He sends them when we need them,
  and His ways are wondrous and wise. . .
So keep looking for an angel
  and keep listening to hear,
For on life's busy, crowded streets,
  you will find God's presence near.

STRANGERS ARE FRIENDS
WE HAVEN'T MET

❦

God knows no strangers, He loves us all,
The poor, the rich, the great, the small.
He is a friend who is always there
To share our troubles and lessen our care.
For no one is a stranger in God's sight,
For God is love, and in His light
May we, too, try in our small way
To make new friends from day to day.
So pass no stranger with an unseeing eye,
For God may be sending a new friend by.

FRIENDS ARE LIFE'S GIFT OF LOVE

If people like me didn't know people like you,
Life would lose its meaning
 and its richness, too. . .
For the friends that we make
 are life's gift of love,
And I think friends are sent
 right from heaven above. . .
And thinking of you somehow makes me feel
That God is love and He's very real.

LIFE IS A GARDEN

Life is a garden,
  good friends are the flowers,
And times spent together
  life's happiest hours. . .
And friendship, like flowers,
  blooms ever more fair
When carefully tended
  by dear friends who care. . .
And life's lovely garden
  would be sweeter by far
If all who passed through it
  were as nice as you are.

THE GOLDEN CHAIN
OF FRIENDSHIP

Friendship is a golden chain,
  the links are friends so dear,
And like a rare and precious jewel,
  it's treasured more each year.
It's clasped together firmly
  with a love that's deep and true,
And it's rich with happy memories
  and fond recollections, too.
Time can't destroy its beauty,
  for as long as memory lives,
Years can't erase the pleasure
  that the joy of friendship gives.
For friendship is a priceless gift
  that can't be bought or sold,
And to have an understanding friend
  is worth far more than gold.
And the golden chain of friendship
  is a strong and blessed tie
Binding kindred hearts together
  as the years go passing by.

THE BLESSINGS OF SHARING

Only what we give away
Enriches us from day to day,
For not in getting but in giving
Is found the lasting joy of living.
For no one ever had a part
In sharing treasures of the heart
Who did not feel the impact of
The magic mystery of God's love.
Love alone can make us kind
And give us joy and peace of mind,
So live with joy unselfishly
And you'll be blessed abundantly.

GIVING IS THE KEY TO LIVING

Every day is a reason for giving
And giving is the key to living. . .
So let us give ourselves away,
Not just today but every day,
And remember, a kind and thoughtful deed
Or a hand outstretched in a time of need
Is the rarest of gifts, for it is a part
Not of the purse but a loving heart. . .
And he who gives of himself will find
True joy of heart and peace of mind.

HEART GIFTS

It's not the things that can be bought
That are life's richest treasures,
It's just the little gifts from the heart
That money cannot measure.
A cheerful smile, a friendly word,
A sympathetic nod,
All priceless little treasures
From the storehouse of our God.
They are the things that can't be bought
With silver or with gold,
For thoughtfulness and kindness
And love are never sold.
They are the priceless things in life
For which no one can pay,
And the giver finds rich recompense
In giving them away.

DEEP IN MY HEART

Happy little memories
  go flitting through my mind,
And in all my thoughts and memories
  I always seem to find
The picture of your face, dear,
  the memory of your touch,
And all the other little things
  I've come to love so much.
You cannot go beyond my thoughts
  or leave my love behind,
Because I keep you in my heart
  and forever on my mind. . .
And though I may not tell you,
  I think you know it's true
That I find daily happiness
  in the very thought of you.

LET GO OF YOUR WORRIES

LET NOT YOUR HEART
BE TROUBLED

Whenever I am troubled
  and lost in deep despair,
I bundle all my troubles up
  and go to God in prayer...
I tell Him I am heartsick
  and lost and lonely, too,
That my mind is deeply burdened,
  and I don't know what to do...
But I know He stilled the tempest
  and calmed the angry sea,
And I humbly ask if, in His love,
  He'll do the same for me...
And then I just keep quiet
  and think only thoughts of peace,
And if I abide in stillness,
  my restless murmurings cease.

AFTER EACH STORM OF LIFE

The rainbow is God's promise
Of hope for you and me,
And though the clouds hang heavy
    and the sun we cannot see,
We know above the dark clouds
    that fill the stormy sky,
Hope's rainbow will come shining through
When the clouds have drifted by.

ADVERSITY CAN BLESS US

The way we use adversity
  is strictly our own choice,
For in God's hands adversity
  can make the heart rejoice.
And while it's very difficult
  for mankind to understand
God's intentions and His purpose
  and the workings of His hand,
If we observe the miracles
  that happen every day,
We cannot help but be convinced
  that in His wondrous way
God makes what seemed unbearable
  and painful and distressing
Easily acceptable when
  we view it as a blessing.

MEET LIFE'S TRIALS
WITH SMILES

There are times when life overwhelms us
And our trials seem too many to bear;
It is then we should stop to remember
God is standing by ready to share
The uncertain hours that confront us
And fill us with fear and despair,
For God in His goodness has promised
That the cross that He gives us to wear
Will never exceed our endurance
Or be more than our strength can bear. . .
And secure in that blessed assurance,
We can smile as we face tomorrow,
For God holds the key to the future,
And no sorrow or care we need borrow.

PATIENCE

Most of the battles of life are won
By looking beyond the clouds to the sun
And having the patience to wait for the day
When the sun comes out
  and the clouds float away.

LIVES DISTRESSED CANNOT
BE BLESSED

❦

Refuse to be discouraged,
  refuse to be distressed,
For when we are despondent,
  our lives cannot be blessed.
For doubt and fear and worry
  close the door to faith and prayer,
And there's no room for blessings
  when we're lost in deep despair.
So remember when you're troubled
  with uncertainty and doubt,
It is best to tell our Father
  what our fear is all about,
For unless we seek His guidance
  when troubled times arise,
We are bound to make decisions
  that are twisted and unwise.
But when we view our problems
  through the eyes of God above,
Misfortunes turn to blessings
  and hatred turns to love.

DAILY PRAYER DISSOLVES YOUR CARES

We all have cares and problems
   we cannot solve alone,
But if we go to God in prayer,
   we are never on our own.
And if we try to stand alone,
   we are weak and we will fall,
For God is always greatest
   when we're helpless, lost, and small. . .
And no day is unmeetable if,
   on rising, our first thought
Is to thank God for the blessings
   that His loving care has brought. . .
And if you follow faithfully
   this daily way to pray,
You will never in your lifetime
   face another hopeless day. . .
For like a soaring eagle,
   you, too, can rise above
The storms of life around you
   on the wings of prayer and love.

BURDENS CAN BE BLESSINGS

Our Father knows what's best for us,
So why should we complain—
We always want the sunshine,
But He knows there must be rain.
We love the sound of laughter
And the merriment of cheer,
But our hearts would lose their tenderness
If we never shed a tear. . .
So whenever we are troubled
And life has lost its song,
It's God testing us with burdens
Just to make our spirit strong!

FAITH ALONE

When the way seems long and the day is dark
And we can't hear the sound
   of the thrush or the lark
And our hearts are heavy with worry and care
And we are lost in the depths of despair,
That is the time when faith alone
Can lead us out of the dark unknown. . .
For faith to believe when the way is rough
And faith to hang on
   when the going is tough
Will never fail to pull us through
And bring us strength and comfort, too. . .
For all we really ever need
Is faith as a grain of mustard seed,
For all God asks is Do you believe?
For if you do ye shall receive.

TROUBLE IS A STEPPING-STONE
TO GROWTH

Trouble is something no one can escape—
Everyone has it in some form or shape.
Some people hide it way down deep inside;
Some people bear it with gallant-like pride.
Some people worry and complain of their lot;
Some people covet what they haven't got.
But the wise man accepts
   whatever God sends,
Willing to yield
   like a storm-tossed tree bends,
Knowing that God never made a mistake,
So whatever He sends
   they are willing to take...
For trouble is part and parcel of life,
And no man can grow
   without struggle or strife.
For the grandeur of life is born of defeat,
For in overcoming we make like complete.

FAITH FOR DARK DAYS

When dark days come—
 and they come to us all—
We feel so helpless and lost and small.
We cannot fathom the reason why,
And it is futile for us to try
To find the answer, the reason or cause,
For the master plan is without any flaws.
And when the darkness shuts out the light,
We must lean on faith to restore our sight,
For there is nothing we need know
If we have faith that wherever we go
God will be there to help us to bear
Our disappointments, pain, and care.
For He is our shepherd,
 our Father, our Guide,
And you're never alone
 with the Lord at your side.
So may the great Physician attend you,
And may His healing completely mend you.

BE OF GOOD CHEER, THERE'S NOTHING TO FEAR

Cheerful thoughts, like sunbeams,
  lighten up the darkest fears,
For when the heart is happy
  there's just no time for tears,
And when the face is smiling
  it's impossible to frown,
And when you are high-spirited
  you cannot feel low-down. . .
For the nature of our attitudes
  toward circumstantial things
Determines our acceptance
  of the problems that life brings. . .
For when the heart is cheerful,
  it cannot be filled with fear,
And without fear, the way ahead
  seems more distinct and clear,
And we realize there's nothing
  that we must face alone,
For our heavenly Father loves us,
  and our problems are His own.

IT'S A WONDERFUL WORLD

In spite of the fact we complain and lament
And view this old world with much discontent,
Deploring conditions and grumbling because
There's so much injustice and so many flaws,
It's a wonderful world, and it's people like you
Who make it that way
  by the things that they do.
For a warm, ready smile
  or a kind, thoughtful deed
Or a hand outstretched in an hour of need
Can change our whole outlook
  and make the world bright,
Where a minute before
  just nothing seemed right.
It's a wonderful world and it always will be
If we keep our eyes open and focused to see
The wonderful things we are capable of
When we open our hearts
  to God and His love.

FAITH IN EVERY SEASON

THE MYSTERY AND MIRACLE
OF HIS CREATIVE HAND

In the beauty of a snowflake
  falling softly on the land
Is the mystery and miracle
  of God's great, creative hand.
What better answers are there
  to prove His holy being
Than the wonders all around us
  that are ours just for the seeing?

THE JOY OF EASTER WAS BORN OF GOOD FRIDAY'S SORROW

Who said the darkness of the night
  would never turn to day?
Who said the winter's bleakness
  would never pass away?
When we know beyond all questioning
  that winter turns to spring
And on the notes of sorrow
  new songs are made to sing?
For no one sheds a teardrop
  or suffers loss in vain,
For God is always there
  to turn our losses into gain...
And every burden borne today
  and every present sorrow
Are but God's happy harbingers
  of a joyous, bright tomorrow.

A TIME OF RENEWAL

No one likes to be sick, and yet we know
It takes sunshine and rain
   to make flowers grow,
And if we never were sick
   and we never felt pain,
We'd be like a desert without any rain.
And who wants a life that is barren and dry
With never a cloud to darken the sky?
For continuous sun goes unrecognized
Like the blessings God sends,
   which are often disguised
For sometimes a sickness
   that seems so distressing
Is a time of renewal and spiritual blessing.

THE SPIRIT OF GIVING

Each year at Christmas, the spirit of giving
Adds joy to the season and gladness to living.
Knowing this happens
  when Christmas is here,
Why can't we continue throughout the year
To make our lives happy
  and abundant with living
By following each day the spirit of giving?

THE SOUL, LIKE NATURE, HAS SEASONS, TOO

Do you ask yourself, as I so often do,
Why must there be days
  that are cheerless and blue?
Why is the song silenced
  in the heart that was gay?
And then I ask God what makes life this way,
And His explanation makes everything clear—
The soul has its seasons the same as the year.
Man, too, must pass through
  life's autumn of death
And have his heart frozen
  by winter's cold breath,
But spring always comes
  with new life and birth,
Followed by summer to warm the soft earth. . .
And oh, what a comfort
  to know there are reasons
That souls, like nature,
  must, too, have their seasons. . .
And it takes a mixture of both bitter and sweet
To season our lives and make them complete.

SPRING AWAKENS WHAT AUTUMN PUTS TO SLEEP

❧

A garden of asters in varying hues,
Crimson pinks and violet blues,
Blossoming in the hazy fall,
Wrapped in autumn's lazy pall. . .
But early frost stole in one night,
And like a chilling, killing blight
It touched each pretty aster's head,
And now the garden's still and dead,
And all the lovely flowers that bloomed
Will soon be buried and entombed
In winter's icy shroud of snow. . .
But oh, how wonderful to know
That after winter comes the spring
To bring new life in everything,
For in God's plan both men and flowers
Can only reach bright, shining hours
By dying first to rise in glory
And prove again the Easter story.

A TIME OF MANY MIRACLES

Flowers sleeping 'neath the snow,
Awakening when the spring winds blow,
Leafless trees so bare before
Gowned in lacy green once more,
Hard, unyielding, frozen sod
Now softly carpeted by God,
Still streams melting in the spring,
Rippling over rocks that sing,
Barren, windswept, lonely hills
Turning gold with daffodils—
These miracles are all around
Within our sight and touch and sound,
As true and wonderful today
As when the stone was rolled away,
Proclaiming to all doubting men
That in God all things live again.

LITTLE SPRINGTIME PRAYER

God, grant me this little springtime prayer
And make our hearts, grown cold with care,
Once more aware of the waking earth
Now pregnant with life
   and bursting with birth.
For how can man feel any fear or doubt
When on every side all around and about
The March winds blow across man's face
And whisper of God's power and grace?
Oh, give us faith to believe again
That peace on earth, goodwill to men
Will follow this winter of man's mind
And awaken his heart and make him kind.
And just as great nature sends the spring
To give new birth to each sleeping thing,
God, grant rebirth to man's slumbering soul
And help him forsake his selfish goal.

GROWING OLDER IS PART OF GOD'S PLAN

You can't hold back the dawn
   or stop the tides from flowing
Or keep a rose from withering
   or still a wind that's blowing,
And time cannot be halted
   in its swift and endless flight,
For age is sure to follow youth
   like day comes after night. . .
For He who sets our span of years
   and watches from above
Replaces youth and beauty
   with peace and truth and love,
And then our souls are privileged
   to see a hidden treasure
That in youth escapes our eyes
   in our pursuit of pleasure. . .
So passing years are but blessings
   that open up the way
To the everlasting beauty
   of God's eternal day.

LIFE'S GOLDEN AUTUMN

Memory opens wide the door
  on a happy day like this,
And with a sweet nostalgia
  we longingly recall,
The happy days of long ago
  that seem the best of all. . .
But time cannot be halted
  in its swift and endless flight,
And age is sure to follow youth
  as day comes after night,
And once again it's proven
  that the restless brain of man
Is powerless to alter God's
  great, unchanging plan. . .
But while our steps grow slower
  and we grow more tired, too,
The soul goes roaring upward
  to realms untouched and new,
Where God's children live forever
  in the beauty of His love.

GOD'S UNFAILING BIRTHDAY PROMISE

❧

From one birthday to another
  God will gladly give
To everyone who seeks Him
  and tries each day to live
A little bit more closely
  to God and to each other,
Seeing everyone who passes
  as a neighbor, friend, or brother,
Not only joy and happiness
  but the faith to meet each trial
Not with fear and trepidation
  but with an inner smile. . .
For we know life's never measured
  by how many years we live
But by the kindly things we do
  and the happiness we give.

THE GOLDEN YEARS OF LIFE

God in His loving and all-wise way
Makes the heart that once
    was too young yesterday
Serene and more gentle and less restless, too,
Content to remember the joys it once knew.
And all that we sought
    on the pathway of pleasure
Becomes but a memory
    to cherish and treasure—
The fast pace grows slower
    and the spirit serene,
And the soul can envision
    what the eyes have not seen.
And so while life's springtime
    is sweet to recall,
The autumn of life is the best time of all,
For our wild youthful yearnings
    all gradually cease,
And God fills our days
    with beauty and peace!

THE BLESSINGS OF
GOD'S SEASONS

We know we must pass
    through the seasons God sends,
Content in the knowledge
    that everything ends,
And oh, what a blessing
    to know there are reasons
And to find that our souls must, too,
    have their seasons—
Bounteous seasons and barren ones, too,
Times for rejoicing and times to be blue—
But meeting these seasons of dark desolation
With the strength that is born of anticipation
Comes from knowing
    that every season of sadness
Will surely be followed
    by a springtime of gladness.

TRIUMPH OVER TRIALS

THE BEND IN THE ROAD

Sometimes we come to life's crossroads
And view what we think is the end,
But God has a much wider vision,
And He knows it's only a bend.
The road will go on and get smoother,
And after we've stopped for a rest,
The path that lies hidden beyond us
Is often the part that is best.
So rest and relax and grow stronger,
Let go and let God share your load
And have faith in a brighter tomorrow;
You've just come to a bend in the road.

GOD BLESS AND KEEP
YOU IN HIS CARE

❧

There are many things in life
   we cannot understand,
But we must trust God's judgment
   and be guided by His hand...
And all who have God's blessing
   can rest safely in His care,
For He promises safe passage
   on the wings of faith and prayer.

WHAT MORE CAN YOU ASK?

God's love endures forever—
What a wonderful thing to know
When the tides of life run against you
And your spirit is downcast and low.
God's kindness is ever around you
Always ready to freely impart
Strength to your faltering spirit,
Cheer to your lonely heart.
God's presence is ever beside you,
As near as the reach of your hand.
You have but to tell Him your troubles—
There is nothing He won't understand.
And knowing God's love is unfailing,
And His mercy unending and great,
You have but to trust in His promise,
"God comes not too soon or too late."
So wait with a heart that is patient
For the goodness of God to prevail,
For never do prayers go unanswered,
And His mercy and love never fail.

TALK IT OVER WITH GOD

You're worried and troubled about everything,
Wondering and fearing
  what tomorrow will bring.
You long to tell someone,
  for you feel so alone,
But your friends are all burdened
  with cares of their own.
There is only one place and only one friend
Who is never too busy,
  and you can always depend
On Him to be waiting, with arms open wide
To hear all the troubles
  you came to confide. . .
For the heavenly Father will always be there
When you seek Him and find Him
  at the altar of prayer.

HOW GREAT THE YIELD FROM A FERTILE FIELD

The farmer plows through the fields of green,
And the blade of the plow is sharp and keen,
But the seed must be sown
   to bring forth grain,
For nothing is born
   without suffering and pain,
And God never plows in the soul of man
Without intention and purpose and plan.
So whenever you feel the plow's sharp blade,
Let not your heart be sorely afraid,
For like the farmer, God chooses a field
From which He expects an excellent yield.
So rejoice though your heart
   be broken in two—
God seeks to bring forth a rich harvest in you.

ANXIOUS PRAYERS

When we are deeply disturbed by a problem
   and our minds are filled with doubt,
And we struggle to find a solution
   but there seems to be no way out...
We kneel down in sheer desperation
   and slowly and stumblingly pray...
But God can't get through to the anxious,
   who are much too impatient to wait,
You have to believe in God's promise
   that He comes not too soon or too late,
For whether God answers promptly
   or delays in answering your prayer,
You must have faith to believe Him
   and to know in your heart He'll be there.
So be not impatient or hasty,
   just trust in the Lord and believe.

NEVER DESPAIR,
GOD'S ALWAYS THERE

In sickness or health,
In suffering and pain,
In storm-laden skies,
In sunshine and rain,
God always is there
To lighten your way
And lead you through darkness
To a much brighter day.

IN GOD OUR STRENGTH

It's a troubled world we live in,
  and we wish that we might find
Not only happiness of heart
  but longed-for peace of mind. . .
But where can we begin our search
  in the age of automation,
With neighbor against neighbor
  and nation against nation,
Where values have no permanence
  and change is all around,
And everything is sinking sand
  and nothing solid ground?
But we've God's Easter promise,
  so let us seek a goal
That opens up new vistas
  for man's eternal soul. . .
For our strength and our security
  lie not in earthly things
But in Christ the Lord, who died for us
  and rose as King of kings.

BLESSINGS DEVISED BY GOD

God speaks to us in many ways,
Altering our lives, our plans, and our days,
And His blessings come in many guises
That He alone in love devises,
And sorrow, which we dread so much,
Can bring a very healing touch. . .
For when we fail to heed His voice
We leave the Lord no other choice
Except to use a firm, stern hand
To make us know He's in command. . .
For on the wings of loss and pain,
The peace we often sought in vain
Will come to us with sweet surprise,
For God is merciful and wise. . .
And through dark hours of tribulation
God gives us time for meditation,
And nothing can be counted loss
Which teaches us to bear our cross.

FAITH AND TRUST

Sometimes when a light
Goes out of our lives
And we are left in darkness
And we do not know which way to go,
We must put our hand
Into the hand of God
And ask Him to lead us
And if we let our lives become a prayer
Until we are strong enough
To stand under the weight
Of our own thoughts again,
Somehow, even the most difficult
Hours are bearable.

FORTRESS OF FAITH

It's easy to say "In God we trust"
   when life is radiant and fair,
But the test of faith is only found
   when there are burdens to bear.
For our claim to faith in the sunshine
   is really no faith at all,
For when roads are smooth and days are bright
   our need for God is so small.
And no one discovers the fullness
   or the greatness of God's love
Unless they have walked in the darkness
   with only a light from above.
For the faith to endure whatever comes
   is born of sorrow and trials
And strengthened only by discipline
   and nurtured by self-denials.
So be not disheartened by troubles,
   for trials are the building blocks
On which to erect a fortress of faith,
   secure on God's ageless rocks.

AFTER THE WINTER, GOD SENDS THE SPRING

Springtime is a season
   of hope and joy and cheer—
There's beauty all around us
   to see and touch and hear. . .
So no matter how downhearted
   and discouraged we may be,
New hope is born when we behold
   leaves budding on a tree
Or when we see a timid flower
   push through the frozen sod
And open wide in glad surprise
   its petaled eyes to God. . .
For this is just God saying,
   "Lift up your eyes to Me,
And the bleakness of your spirit,
   like the budding springtime tree,
Will lose its wintry darkness
   and your heavy heart will sing."
For God never sends the winter
   without the joy of spring.

THE COMFORT AND SWEETNESS OF PEACE

After the clouds, the sunshine,
After the winter, the spring,
After the shower, the rainbow—
For life is a changeable thing.
After the night, the morning,
Bidding all darkness cease,
After life's cares and sorrows,
The comfort and sweetness of peace.

TRUST IN GOD'S PLAN

THY WILL BE DONE

God did not promise sun without rain,
Light without darkness, or joy without pain.
He only promised strength for the day
When the darkness comes
  and we lose our way...
For only through sorrow
  do we grow more aware
That God is our refuge in times of despair.
For then we seek shelter
  in His wondrous love,
And we ask him to send us help from above...
And that is the reason we know it is true
That bright shining hours
  and dark, sad ones, too,
Are part of the plan God made for each one,
And all we can pray is "Thy will be done."
And know that you are never alone,
For God is your Father
  and you're one of His own.

THE HOME BEYOND

We feel so sad when those we love
Are called to live in the home above,
But why should we grieve
    when they say good-bye
And go to dwell in a cloudless sky?
For they have but gone to prepare the way,
And we'll meet them again some happy day,
For God has told us that nothing can sever
A life He created to live forever.
So let God's promise soften our sorrow
And give us new strength
    for a brighter tomorrow.

GOD'S HAND IS ALWAYS THERE

I am perplexed and often vexed,
And sometimes I cry and sadly sigh,
But do not think, dear Father above,
That I question You or Your unfailing love.
It's just that sometimes when I reach out,
You seem to be nowhere about.
And while I'm sure You love me still,
I know in my heart that You always will,
Somehow I feel I cannot reach You.
And though I get on my knees
    and beseech You,
I cannot bring You close to me,
And I feel adrift on life's raging sea.
But though I cannot find your hand
To lead me on to the promised land,
I still believe with all my being
Your hand is there beyond my seeing.

YOU ARE NEVER ALONE

There's truly nothing we need know
If we have faith wherever we go.
God will be there to help us bear
Our disappointments, pain, and care,
For He is our shepherd, our Father, our guide.
You're never alone with the Lord at your side.

HE UNDERSTANDS

Although it sometimes seems to us
  our prayers have not been heard,
God always knows our every need
  without a single word,
And he will not forsake us
  even though the way is steep,
For always He is near to us,
  a tender watch to keep.
And in good time he will answer us,
  and in His love He'll send
Greater things than we have asked
  and blessings without end.
So though we do not understand
  why trouble comes to man,
Can we not be contented
  just to know it is God's plan?

TRUST GOD

Take heart and meet each minute
   with faith in God's great love,
Aware that every day of life
   is controlled by God above...
And never dread tomorrow
   or what the future brings—
Just pray for strength and courage
   and trust God in all things.

THIS, TOO, WILL PASS AWAY

If I can endure for this minute
Whatever is happening to me
No matter how heavy my heart is
Or how dark the moment may be—
If I can remain calm and quiet
With all my world crashing about me,
Secure in the knowledge God loves me
When everyone else seems to doubt me—
If I can but keep on believing
What I know in my heart to be true,
That darkness will fade with the morning
And that this will pass away, too,
Then nothing in life can defeat me,
For as long as this knowledge remains,
I can suffer whatever is happening,
For I know God will break all the chains
That are binding me tight in the darkness
And trying to fill me with fear. . .
For there is no night without dawning,
And I know that my morning is near.

STEPPING-STONES TO GOD

An aching heart is but a stepping-stone
To greater joy than you've ever known,
For things that cause the heart to ache
Until you think that it must break
Become the strength by which we climb
To higher heights that are sublime
And feel the radiance of God's smiles
When we have soared above life's trials.
So when you're overwhelmed with fears
And all your hopes are drenched in tears,
Think not that life has been unfair
And given you too much to bear,
For God has chosen you because,
With all your weaknesses and flaws,
He feels that you are worthy of
The greatness of His wondrous love.

GOD'S SWEETEST
APPOINTMENTS

Out of life's misery born of man's sins,
A fuller, richer life begins,
For when we are helpless with no place to go
And our hearts are heavy
    and our spirits are low,
If we place our lives in God's hands
And surrender completely
    to His will and demands,
The darkness lifts and the sun shines through,
And by His touch we are born anew.
For with patience to wait and faith to endure,
Your life will be blessed
    and your future secure.
For God is but testing
    your faith and your love
Before He appoints you to rise far above
All the small things that so sorely distress you,
For God's only intention
    is to strengthen and bless you.

WE CAN'T, BUT GOD CAN

Why things happen as they do
  we do not always know,
And we cannot always fathom
  why our spirits sink so low.
We flounder in our dark distress,
  we are wavering and unstable,
But when we're most inadequate,
  the Lord God's always able—
For though we are incapable,
  God is powerful and great,
And there's no darkness of the mind
  God cannot penetrate.
And in His time, if we have faith,
  He will gradually restore
The brightness to our spirits
  that we've been longing for.
So remember there's no cloud too dark
  for God's light to penetrate
If we keep on believing
  and have faith enough to wait.

BEYOND OUR ASKING

More than hearts can imagine
  or minds comprehend,
God's bountiful gifts are ours without end.
We ask for a cupful when the vast sea is ours,
We pick a small rosebud
  from a garden of flowers,
We reach for a sunbeam
  but the sun still abides,
We draw one short breath
  but there's air on all sides.
Whatever we ask for
  falls short of God's giving,
For His greatness exceeds every facet of living,
And always God's ready and eager and willing
To pour out His mercy, completely fulfilling
All of man's needs for peace, joy, and rest,
For God gives His children whatever is best.
For God has a storehouse just filled to the brim
With all that man needs if we'll only ask Him.

IN HIM WE LIVE AND MOVE
AND HAVE OUR BEING

We walk in a world
  that is strange and unknown,
And in the midst of the crowd
  we still feel alone.
We question our purpose,
  our part, and our place
In this vast land of mystery
  suspended in space.
We probe and explore and try hard to explain
The tumult of thoughts
  that our minds entertain. . .
Unable to fathom what tomorrow will bring,
But there is one truth to which we can cling. . .
For while life's a mystery man can't understand,
The great Giver of life is holding our hands,
And safe in His care
  there is no need for seeing,
"For in Him we live and move
  and have our being."

THIS IS JUST A RESTING PLACE

Sometimes the road of life seems long
   as we travel through the years,
And with a heart that's broken
   and eyes brimful of tears,
We falter in our weariness
   and sink beside the way,
But God leans down and whispers,
   "Child, there'll be another day,"
And the road will grow much smoother
   and much easier to face,
So do not be disheartened;
   this is just a resting place.

DAILY
THANKSGIVING

THANK YOU, GOD, FOR EVERYTHING

⤜⤛

Thank You, God, for everything—
    the big things and the small—
For every good gift comes from God,
    the Giver of them all,
And all too often we accept
    without any thanks or praise
The gifts God sends as blessings
    each day in many ways.
And so at this time we offer up a prayer
To thank You, God, for giving us
    a lot more than our share.
First, thank You for the little things
    that often come our way—
The things we take for granted
    and don't mention when we pray—
Oh, make us more aware, dear God,
    of little daily graces
That come to us with sweet surprise
    from never-dreamed-of places.
And help us to remember that
    the key to life and living
Is to make each prayer a prayer of thanks
    and each day a day of thanksgiving.

COUNT YOUR GAINS,
NOT LOSSES

As we travel down life's busy road
Complaining of our heavy load,
We often think God's been unfair
And given us much more than our share
Of daily, little irritations
And disappointing tribulations.
Our troubles fill our every thought;
We dwell upon the goals we sought,
And so we walk with heads held low,
And little do we guess or know
That someone near us on life's street
Is burdened deeply with defeat,
And if we'd but forget our care
And stop in sympathy to share
The burden that our brother carried,
Our minds and hearts would be less harried
And we would feel our load was small—
In fact, we carried no load at all.

A THANKFUL HEART

Take nothing for granted,
   for whenever you do,
The joy of enjoying is lessened for you.
For we rob our own lives
   much more than we know
When we fail to respond or in any way show
Our thanks for the blessings
   that daily are ours—
The warmth of the sun,
   the fragrances of flowers,
The beauty of twilight, the freshness of dawn,
The coolness of dew on a green velvet lawn,
The kind little deeds so thoughtfully done,
The favors of friends
   and the love that someone
Unselfishly gives us in a myriad of ways,
Expecting no payment
   and no words of praise.
For the joy of enjoying
   and the fullness of living
Are found in the heart
   that is filled with thanksgiving.

SO MANY REASONS TO
LOVE THE LORD

❧

Thank You, God, for little things
   that come unexpectedly
To brighten up a dreary day
   that dawned so dismally.
Oh God, the list is endless
   of the things to thank You for,
But I take them all for granted
   and unconsciously ignore
That everything I think or do,
   each movement that I make,
Each measured, rhythmic heartbeat,
   each breath of life I take
Is something You have given me
   for which there is no way
For me in all my smallness
   to in any way repay.

THINGS TO BE THANKFUL FOR

The good, green earth beneath our feet,
The air we breathe, the food we eat,
Some work to do, a goal to win,
A hidden longing deep within
That spurs us on to bigger things
And helps us meet what each day brings—
All these things and many more
Are things we should be thankful for...
And most of all, our thankful prayers
Should rise to God because He cares.

A HEART FULL OF THANKSGIVING

Everyone needs someone to be thankful for,
And each day of life
   we are aware of this more,
For the joy of enjoying
   and the fullness of living
Are found only in hearts
   that are filled with thanksgiving.

THE HAND OF GOD IS EVERYWHERE

❧

It's true we have never looked on His face,
But His likeness shines forth
   from every place,
For the hand of God is everywhere
Along life's busy thoroughfare,
And His presence can be felt and seen
Right in the midst of our daily routine.
Things we touch and see and feel
Are what make God so very real.

FOREVER THANKS

Give thanks for the blessings
　　that daily are ours—
The warmth of the sun,
　　the fragrance of flowers.
With thanks for all the thoughtful,
　　caring things you always do
And a loving wish for happiness
　　today and all year through!

WARM OUR HEARTS
WITH THY LOVE

Oh God, who made the summer
   and warmed the earth with beauty,
Warm our hearts with gratitude
   and devotion to our duty.
For in this age of violence,
   rebellion, and defiance,
We've forgotten the true meaning
   of dependable reliance.
Our standards have been lowered,
   and we resist all discipline,
And our vision has been narrowed
   and blinded to all sin.
Oh God, look down on our cold hearts
   and warm them with Your love,
And grant us Your forgiveness
   which we're so unworthy of.

WORDS CAN SAY SO LITTLE

Today is an occasion
   for compliments and praise
And saying many of the things
   we don't say other days.
For often through the passing days
   we feel deep down inside
Unspoken thoughts of thankfulness
   and fond, admiring pride.
But words can say so little
   when the heart is overflowing,
And often those we love the most
   just have no way of knowing
The many things the heart conceals
   and never can impart,
For words seem so inadequate
   to express what's in the heart.

NOT BY CHANCE OR HAPPENSTANCE

Into our lives come many things
    to break the dull routine—
The things we had not planned
    or that happen unforeseen,
The unexpected little joys
    that are scattered on our way,
Success we did not count on
    or a rare, fulfilling day,
The sudden, unplanned meeting
    that comes with sweet surprise
And lights the heart with happiness
    like a rainbow in the skies.
And every lucky happening
    and every lucky break
Are little gifts from God above
    that are ours to freely take.

MEET GOD IN THE MORNING

Each day at dawning
  I lift my heart high
And raise up my eyes
  to the infinite sky.
I watch the night vanish
  as a new day is born,
And I hear the birds sing
  on the wings of the morn.
I see the dew glisten
  in crystal-like splendor
While God, with a touch
  that is gentle and tender,
Wraps up the night
  and softly tucks it away
And hangs out the sun
  to herald a new day.
And so I give thanks
  and my heart kneels to pray,
"God, keep me and guide me
  and go with me today."

A PRAYER OF THANKS

⁓

Thank You, God, for the beauty
  around me everywhere,
The gentle rain and glistening dew,
  the sunshine and the air,
The joyous gift of feeling
  the soul's soft, whispering voice
That speaks to me from deep within
  and makes my heart rejoice.

NATURE'S
ENCOURAGEMENT

THIS IS MY FATHER'S WORLD

❦

Everywhere across the land
You see God's face and touch His hand.
Each time you look up in the sky,
Or watch the fluffy clouds drift by,
Or feel the sunshine, warm and bright,
Or watch the dark night turn to light,
Or hear a bluebird brightly sing,
Or see the winter turn to spring,
Or stop to pick a daffodil,
Or gather violets on some hill,
Or touch a leaf or see a tree,
It's all God whispering, "This is Me. . .
And I am faith and I am light
And in Me there shall be no night."

IN GOD'S TOMORROW THERE
IS ETERNAL SPRING

All nature heeds the call of spring
  as God awakens everything,
And all that seemed so dead and still
  experiences a sudden thrill
As springtime lays a magic hand
  across God's vast and fertile land.
Oh, the joy in standing by to watch
  a sapphire springtime sky
Or see a fragile flower break through
  what just a day ago or two
Seemed barren ground still hard with frost,
  for in God's world, no life is lost,
And flowers sleep beneath the ground,
  but when they hear spring's waking sound,
They push themselves through layers of clay
  to reach the sunlight of God's day.
And man and woman, like flowers, too,
  must sleep until called
  from the darkened deep
To live in that place where angels sing
  and where there is eternal spring.

NOTHING IS LOST FOREVER

The waking earth in springtime
Reminds us it is true
That nothing ever really dies
That is not born anew...
So trust God's all-wise wisdom
And doubt the Father never,
For in His heavenly kingdom
There is nothing lost forever.

MY GARDEN OF PRAYER

My garden beautifies my yard
  and adds fragrance to the air,
But it is also my cathedral
  and my quiet place of prayer.
So little do we realize that
  the glory and the power
Of Him who made the universe
  lies hidden in a flower!

EACH SPRING GOD RENEWS
HIS PROMISE

Long, long ago in a land far away,
There came the dawn of the first Easter day,
And each year we see the promise reborn
That God gave the world
  on that first Easter morn.
For in each waking flower
  and each singing bird
The promise of Easter is witnessed and heard,
And spring is God's way of speaking to men
And renewing the promise of Easter again. . .
For death is a season
  that man must pass through,
And just like the flowers, God wakens him, too.
So why should we grieve
  when our loved ones die,
For we'll meet them again in a cloudless sky.
For Easter is more than a beautiful story—
It's the promise of life and eternal glory.

I COME TO MEET YOU

I come to meet You, God, and as I linger here
I seem to feel You very near.
A rustling leaf, a rolling slope
Speak to my heart of endless hope.
The sun just rising in the sky,
The waking birdlings as they fly,
The grass all wet with morning dew
Are telling me I just met You.
And gently thus the day is born
As night gives way to breaking morn,
And once again I've met You, God,
And worshipped on Your holy sod.
For who could see the dawn break through
Without a glimpse of heaven and You?
For who but God could make the day
And softly put the night away?

FULFILLMENT

Apple blossoms bursting wide
  now beautify a tree
And make a springtime picture
  that is beautiful to see.
Oh fragrant, lovely blossoms,
  you'll make a bright bouquet
If I but break your branches
  from the apple tree today,
But if I but break your branches
  and make your beauty mine,
You'll bear no fruit in season
  when severed from the vine,
And when we cut ourselves away
  from guidance that's divine,
Our lives will be as fruitless
  as the branch without the vine.
For as the flowering branches
  depend upon the tree
To nourish and fulfill them
  till they reach futurity,
We, too, must be dependent
  on our Father up above,
For we are but the branches,
  and He's the tree of love.

THE HEAVENS DECLARE THE GLORY OF GOD

You ask me how I know it's true
That there is a living God
A God who rules the universe—
The sky, the sea, the sod—
A God who holds all creatures
In the hollow of His hand,
A God who put infinity
In one tiny grain of sand,
A God who made the seasons—
Winter, summer, fall, and spring—
And put His flawless rhythm
Into each created thing,
A God who hangs the sun out
Slowly with the break of day
And gently takes the stars in
And puts the night away...
What better answers are there
To prove His holy being
Than the wonders all around us
That are ours just for the seeing.

THE MASTERPIECE

Framed by the vast, unlimited sky,
Bordered by mighty waters,
Sheltered by beautiful woodland groves,
Scented with flowers that bloom and die,
Protected by giant mountain peaks—
The land of the great unknown—
Snowcapped and towering, a nameless place
That beckons man on as the gold he seeks,
Bubbling with life and earthly joys,
Reeking with pain and mortal strife,
Dotted with wealth and material gains,
Built on ideals of girls and boys,
Streaked with toil,
    opportunity's banner unfurled
Stands out the masterpiece of art
Painted by the one great God,
A picture of the world.

THE AUTUMN OF LIFE

What a wonderful time is life's autumn,
 when the leaves of the trees are all gold,
When God fills each day as He sends it
 with memories priceless and old.
What a treasure house filled with rare jewels
 are the blessings of year upon year,
When life has been lived as you've lived it
 in a home where God's presence is near. . .
May the deep meaning surrounding this day,
 like the paintbrush of God up above,
Touch your life with wonderful blessings.

FINDING FAITH IN A FLOWER

Sometimes when faith is running low
And I cannot fathom why things are so,
I walk among the flowers that grow
And learn the answers to all I would know. . .
For among my flowers I have come to see
Life's miracle and its mystery,
And standing in silence and reverie,
My faith comes flooding back to me.

APPRIL

April comes with cheeks a-glowing
Silver streams are all a-flowing,
Flowers open wide their eyes
In lovely rapturous surprise.
Lilies dream beside the brooks,
Violets in meadow nooks,
And the birds gone wild with glee
Fill the woods with melody.

LISTEN IN SILENCE IF YOU WOULD HEAR

Silently the green leaves grow,
In silence falls the soft, white snow,
Silently the flowers bloom,
In silence sunshine fills a room.
Silently bright stars appear,
In silence velvet night draws near,
And silently God enters in
To free a troubled heart from sin.

PEACE AND QUIET
IN HIM

THE FIRST THING EVERY MORNING AND THE LAST THING EVERY NIGHT

Were you too busy this morning
To quietly stop and pray?
Did you hurry and drink your coffee
Then frantically rush away,
Consoling yourself by saying,
God will always be there
Waiting to hear my petitions,
Ready to answer each prayer?
It's true that the great, generous Savior
Forgives our transgressions each day
And patiently waits for lost sheep
Who constantly seem to stray. . .
For only through prayer that's unhurried
Can the needs of the day be met,
And only through prayers said at evening
Can we sleep without fears or regret.
So seek the Lord in the morning
And never forget Him at night,
For prayer is an unfailing blessing
That makes every burden seem light.

HE ASKS SO LITTLE AND
GIVES SO MUCH

✑

What must I do to ensure peace of mind?
Is the answer I'm seeking too hard to find?
How can I know what God wants me to be?
How can I tell what's expected of me?
Where can I go for guidance and aid
To help me correct the errors I've made?
The answer is found in doing three things,
And great is the gladness
   that doing them brings.
"Do justice"—"Love kindness"—
   "Walk humbly with God"—
For with these three things
   as your rule and your rod,
All things worth having are yours to achieve,
If you follow God's words
   and have faith to believe.

EXPECTATION! ANTICIPATION! REALIZATION!

God gives us a power we so seldom employ,
For we're so unaware it is filled with such joy.
The gift that God gives us is anticipation,
Which we can fulfill with sincere expectation,
For there's power in belief
   when we think we will find
Joy for the heart and peace for the mind,
And believing the day will bring a surprise
Is not only pleasant but surprisingly wise. . .
For we open the door to let joy walk through
When we learn to expect
   the best and the most, too,
And believing we'll find a happy surprise
Makes reality out of a fancied surmise.

IT'S ME AGAIN, GOD

Remember me, God?
　I come every day
Just to talk with You, Lord,
　and to learn how to pray.
You make me feel welcome;
　You reach out Your hand.
I need never explain,
　for You understand.
I come to You frightened
　and burdened with care,
So lonely and lost and
　so filled with despair,
And suddenly, Lord,
　I'm no longer afraid—
My burden is lighter
　and the dark shadows fade.
Oh God, what a comfort
　to know that You care
And to know when I seek You,
　You will always be there.

NO FAVOR DO I SEEK TODAY

I come not to ask,
   to plead or implore You—
I just come to tell You
   how much I adore You.
For to kneel in Your presence
   makes me feel blessed,
For I know that You know
   all my needs best,
And it fills me with joy
   just to linger with You
As my soul You replenish
   and my heart You renew.
For prayer is much more
   than just asking for things—
It's the peace and contentment
   that quietness brings.
So thank You again
   for Your mercy and love
And for making me heir
   to Your kingdom above.

INSPIRATION! MEDITATION! DEDICATION!

Brighten your day
And lighten your way
And lessen your cares
With daily prayers.
Quiet your mind
And leave tension behind
And find inspiration
In hushed meditation.

LEARN TO REST

We all need short vacations
   in life's fast and maddening race
An interlude of quietness
   from the constant, jet-age pace,
So when your day is pressure-packed
   and your hours are all too few,
Just close your eyes and meditate
   and let God talk to you.
Just close your eyes in silent prayer
   and ask the Lord to bless
Each thought that you are thinking,
   each decision you must make,
As well as every word you speak
   and every step you take
For only by the grace of God
   can you gain self-control,
And only meditative thoughts
   can restore your peace and soul.

A MEDITATION

God in His loving and all-wise way
Makes the heart that once was
  too young yesterday
Serene and more gentle and less restless, too,
Content to remember
  the joys it once knew. . .
And all that we sought
  on the pathway of pleasure
Becomes but a memory
  to cherish and treasure—
The fast pace grows slower
  and the spirit serene,
And the soul can envision
  what the eyes have not seen. . .
And so while life's springtime
  is sweet to recall,
The autumn of life is the best time of all,
For our wild youthful yearnings
  all gradually cease
And God fills our days
  with beauty and peace!

GOD IS NO STRANGER

God is no stranger in a faraway place;
He's as close as the wind
    that blows 'cross my face.
It's true I can't see the wind as it blows,
But I feel it around me,
    and my heart surely knows
That God's mighty hand can be felt everywhere,
For there's nothing on earth
    that is not in God's care.
The sky and the stars, the waves and the sea,
The dew on the grass, the leaves on a tree
Are constant reminders
    of God and His nearness,
Proclaiming His presence
    with crystal-like clearness.
So how could I think God was far, far away
When I feel Him beside me
    every hour of the day?
And I've plenty of reasons
    to know God's my friend,
And this is one friendship that time cannot end.

LISTEN IN THE QUIETNESS

To try to run away from life
　is impossible to do,
For no matter where you chance to go,
　your troubles will follow you;
For though the scenery is different,
　when you look deep inside you'll find
The same deep, restless longings
　that you thought you left behind.
So when life becomes a problem
　much too great for us to bear,
Instead of trying to escape,
　let us withdraw in prayer.
For withdrawal means renewal
　if we withdraw to pray
And listen in the quietness
　to hear what God will say.

THE PEACE OF MEDITATION

So we may know God better
  and feel His quiet power,
Let us daily keep in silence
  a meditation hour.
For to understand God's greatness
  and to use His gifts each day,
The soul must learn to meet Him
  in a meditative way.
For our Father tells His children
  that if they would know His will
They must seek Him in the silence
  when all is calm and still.
For when everything is quiet
  and we're lost in meditation,
Our souls are then preparing
  for a deeper dedication
That will make it wholly possible
  to quietly endure
The violent world around us,
  for in God we are secure.

A PRAYER FOR PEACE
AND PATIENCE

God, teach me to be patient,
  teach me to go slow.
Teach me how to wait on You
  when my way I do not know.
Teach me sweet forbearance,
  when things do not go right,
So I remain unruffled
  when others grow uptight.
Teach me how to quiet
  my racing, rising heart,
So I might hear the answer
  You are trying to impart.
Teach me to let go, dear God,
  and pray undisturbed until
My heart is filled with inner peace
  and I learn to know Your will.

WIDEN MY VISION

God, open my eyes so I may see
And feel Your presence close to me.
Give me strength for my stumbling feet
As I battle the crowd on life's busy street,
And widen the vision of my unseeing eyes
So in passing faces I'll recognize
Not just a stranger, unloved and unknown,
But a friend with a heart
    that is much like my own.
Give me perception to make me aware
That scattered profusely on life's thoroughfare
Are the best gifts of God that we daily pass by
As we look at the world with an unseeing eye.

CHOOSING JOY

SEEK FIRST THE KINGDOM
OF GOD

Life is a mixture of sunshine and rain,
Good things and bad things, pleasure and pain.
We can't have all sunshine, but it's certainly true
That there's never a cloud
    the sun doesn't shine through. . .
So always remember, whatever betide you,
The power of God is always beside you. . .
Take heart and stand tall and think who you are,
For God is your Father and no one can bar
Or keep you from reaching your desired success
Or withhold the joy that is yours to possess. . .
For you need nothing more
    than God's guidance and love
To ensure you the things
    that you're most worthy of. . .
So trust in His wisdom and follow His ways
And be not concerned
    with the world's empty praise,
But first seek His kingdom and you will possess
The world's greatest of riches,
    which is true happiness.

BRIGHTEN THE CORNER
WHERE YOU ARE

We cannot all be famous or listed in *Who's Who*,
But every person, great or small,
   has important work to do...
For it's not the big celebrity
   in a world of fame and praise,
But it's doing unpretentiously
   in undistinguished ways
The work that God assigned to us,
   unimportant as it seems,
That makes our task outstanding
   and brings reality to dreams...
For if everybody brightened up
   the spot on which they're standing
By being more considerate
   and a little less demanding,
This dark old world would very soon
   eclipse the evening star
If everybody brightened up
   the corner where they are.

GOD'S ASSURANCE GIVES US ENDURANCE

My blessings are so many,
  my troubles are so few,
How can I be discouraged
  when I know that I have You?
And I have the sweet assurance
  that there's nothing I need fear
If I but keep remembering
  I am Yours and You are near.
Help me to endure the storms
  that keep raging deep inside me,
And make me more aware each day
  that no evil can betide me.
If I remain undaunted
  though the billows sweep and roll,
Knowing I have Your assurance,
  there's a haven for my soul,
For anything and everything
  can somehow be endured
If Your presence is beside me
  and lovingly assured.

WORRY NO MORE—GOD
KNOWS THE SCORE

Have you ever been caught
  in a web you didn't weave,
Involved in conditions
  that are hard to believe?
Have you ever felt you must
  speak and explain and deny
A story that's groundless
  or a small, whispered lie?
Well, don't be upset,
  for God knows the score,
And with God as your judge
  you need worry no more...
And knowing that God
  is your judge and your jury
Frees you completely
  from man's falseness and fury...
And secure in this knowledge,
  let your thoughts rise above
Man's small, shallow judgments
  that are so empty of
God's goodness and greatness in judging men,
And forget ugly rumors and be happy again.

YOUR LIFE WILL BE BLESSED IF
YOU LOOK FOR THE BEST

It's easy to grow downhearted
  when nothing goes your way,
It's easy to be discouraged
  when you have a troublesome day,
But trouble is only a challenge
  to spur you on to achieve
The best that God has to offer,
  if you have the faith to believe!

TAKE TIME TO BE KIND

Kindness is a virtue given by the Lord—
It pays dividends in happiness
    and joy is its reward.
For if you practice kindness
    in all you say and do,
The Lord will wrap His kindness
    around your heart and you.

WHAT IS LIFE?

Life is a sojourn here on earth
Which begins the day God gives us birth.
We enter this world from the great unknown,
And God gives each spirit a form of its own
And endows this form with a heart and a soul
To spur man on to his ultimate goal. . .
And through the senses of feeling and seeing,
God makes man into a human being
So he may experience a mortal life
And through this period of smiles and strife
Prepare himself to return as he came,
For birth and death are in essence the same,
So enjoy your sojourn on earth and be glad
That God gives you a choice
    between good things and bad,
And only be sure that you heed God's voice
Whenever life asks you to make a choice.

IN HOURS OF DISCOURAGEMENT, GOD IS OUR ENCOURAGEMENT

Sometimes we feel uncertain
  and unsure of everything,
Afraid to make decisions,
  dreading what the day will bring.
God has given us the answers,
  which too often go unheeded,
But if we search His promises
  we'll find everything that's needed
To lift our faltering spirits
  and renew our courage, too,
For there's absolutely nothing
  too much for God to do...
So cast your burden on Him,
  seek His counsel when distressed,
And go to Him for comfort
  when you're lonely and oppressed...
For in God is our encouragement
  in trouble and in trials,
And in suffering and in sorrow
  He will turn our tears to smiles.

THE CALL TO REJOICE

My cross is not too heavy,
  my road is not too rough
Because God walks beside me,
  and to know this is enough...
And though I get so lonely,
  I know I'm not alone,
For the Lord God is my Father
  and He loves me as His own...
So though I'm tired and weary
  and I wish my race were run,
God will only terminate it
  when my work on earth is done...
So let me stop complaining
  about my load of care,
For God will always lighten it
  when it gets too much to bear...
And if He does not ease my load,
  He'll give me strength to bear it,
For God, in love and mercy,
  is always near to share it.

LOOK ON THE SUNNY SIDE

There are always two sides
    the good and the bad,
The dark and the light, the sad and the glad.
So thank God for the good things
    He has already done,
And be grateful to Him
    for the battles you've won
And know that the same God
    who helped you before
Is ready and willing
    to help you once more.
For our Father in heaven
    always knows what is best,
And if you trust His wisdom,
    your life will be blessed.
For always remember that whatever betide you,
You are never alone, for God is beside you.

BLESSINGS COME IN
MANY GUISES

～～

When troubles come and things go wrong
And days are cheerless and nights are long,
We find it so easy to give in to despair
By magnifying the burdens we bear.
We add to our worries by refusing to try
To look for the rainbow in an overcast sky,
And the blessings God sent
   in a darkened disguise
Our troubled hearts fail to recognize,
Not knowing God sent it not to distress us
But to strengthen our faith
   and redeem us and bless us.

THE FRAGRANCE REMAINS

There's an old Chinese proverb
  that if practiced each day
Would change the whole world
  in a wonderful way.
Its truth is so simple, it's easy to do,
And it works every time and successfully, too.
For you can't do a kindness without a reward
Not in silver nor gold
  but in joy from the Lord.
You can't light a candle to show others the way
Without feeling the warmth
  of that bright little ray,
And you can't pluck a rose
  all fragrant with dew
Without part of its fragrance
  remaining with you.

THE JOY OF UNSELFISH GIVING

Time is not measured
  by the years that you live
But by the deeds that you do
  and the joy that you give.
And from birthday to birthday,
  the good Lord above
Bestows on His children the gift of His love,
Asking us only to share it with others
By treating all people
  not as strangers but brothers.
And each day as it comes
  brings a chance to each one
To live to the fullest, leaving nothing undone
That would brighten the life
  or lighten the load
Of some weary traveler lost on life's road.
So it doesn't matter how long we may live
If as long as we live we unselfishly give.

THE NECESSITY
OF PRAYER

BEGIN EACH DAY BY KNEELING TO PRAY

Start every day with a "good morning" prayer
And God will bless each thing you do
And keep you in His care...
And never, never sever
  the spirit's silken strand
That our Father up in heaven
  holds in his mighty hand.

ANYWHERE IS A PLACE OF PRAYER IF GOD IS THERE

I have prayed on my knees in the morning,
 I have prayed as I walked along,
I have prayed in the silence and darkness,
 and I've prayed to the tune of a song.
But often I had the feeling
 that my prayers were not getting through...
And I realized then that our Father
 is not really concerned when we pray
Or impressed by our manner of worship
 or the eloquent words that we say.
He is only concerned with our feelings,
 and He looks deep down into our hearts
And hears the cry of our souls' deep need
 that no words could ever impart...
So it isn't the prayer that's expressive
 or offered in some special spot
That's the sincere plea of a sinner,
 and God can tell whether or not
We honestly seek His forgiveness
 and earnestly mean what we say,
And then and then only God answers
 the prayers that we fervently pray.

WISH NOT FOR EASE OR TO DO AS YOU PLEASE

If wishes worked like magic
   and plans worked that way, too,
And if everything you wished for,
   whether good or bad for you,
Immediately were granted
   with no effort on your part,
You'd experience no fulfillment
   of your spirit or your heart.
For things achieved too easily
   lose their charm and meaning, too,
For it is life's difficulties
   and the trial times we go through
That make us strong in spirit
   and endow us with the will
To surmount the insurmountable
   and to climb the highest hill.
So wish not for the easy way
   to win your heart's desire,
For the joy's in overcoming
   and withstanding flood and fire,
For to triumph over trouble
   and grow stronger with defeat
Is to win the kind of victory
   that will make your life complete.

NOT WHAT YOU WANT, BUT
WHAT GOD WILLS

Do you want what you want when you want it,
Do you pray and expect a reply?
And when it's not instantly answered,
Do you feel that God passed you by?
Well, prayers that are prayed in this manner
Are really not prayers at all,
For you can't go to God in a hurry
And expect Him to answer your call.
For prayers are not meant for obtaining
What we selfishly wish to acquire,
For God in His wisdom refuses
The things that we wrongly desire...
And don't pray for freedom from trouble
Or pray that life's trials pass you by.
Instead pray for strength and for courage
To meet life's dark hours and not cry
That God was not there when you called Him
And He turned a deaf ear to your prayer
And just when you need Him most of all
He left you alone in despair.

MY DAILY PRAYER

God, be my resting place and my protection
In hours of trouble, defeat, and dejection.
May I never give way to self-pity and sorrow,
May I always be sure of a better tomorrow,
May I stand undaunted come what may,
Secure in the knowledge I have only to pray
And ask my Creator and Father above
To keep me serene in His grace and His love.

POWER OF PRAYER

I am only a worker employed by the Lord,
And great is my gladness and rich my reward
If I can just spread the wonderful story
That God is the answer to eternal glory. . .
Bringing new hope and comfort and cheer,
Telling sad hearts there is nothing to fear,
And what greater joy
    could there be than to share
The love of God and the power of prayer.

DAILY PRAYERS ARE HEAVEN'S STAIRS

❧

The stairway rises heaven-high,
  the steps are dark and steep.
In weariness we climb them
  as we stumble, fall, and weep.
And many times we falter
  along the path of prayer,
Wondering if You hear us
  and if You really care.
Oh, give us some assurance;
  restore our faith anew,
So we can keep on climbing
  the stairs of prayer to You.
For we are weak and wavering,
  uncertain and unsure,
And only meeting You in prayer
  can help us to endure
All life's trials and troubles,
  its sickness, pain, and sorrow,
And give us strength and courage
  to face and meet tomorrow.

THE HEAVENLY STAIRCASE

Prayers are the stairs that lead to God
And there's joy every step of the way
When we make our pilgrimage to Him
With love in our hearts each day.

SHOW ME MORE CLEARLY
THE WAY TO SERVE
AND LOVE YOU MORE
EACH DAY

❧

God, help me in my feeble way
To somehow do something each day
To show You that I love You best
And that my faith will stand each test,
And let me serve You every day
And feel You near me when I pray.
Oh, hear my prayer, dear God above,
And make me worthy of Your love.

GOD IS THE ANSWER

We read the headlines daily;
  and we listen to the news;
We are anxious and bewildered
  with the world's conflicting views.
So instead of reading headlines
  that disturb the heart and mind,
Let us open up the Bible,
  for in doing so we'll find
That this age is no different
  from the millions gone before,
And in every hour of crisis
  God has opened up a door.
So as we pray for guidance,
  may a troubled world revive
Faith in God and confidence
  so our nation may survive
And draw us even closer
  to God and to each other
Until every stranger is a friend
  and every man a brother.

THE HOUSE OF PRAYER

Just close your eyes and open your heart
And feel your cares and worries depart.
Just yield yourself to the Father above
And let Him hold you secure in His love. . .
So when you are tired, discouraged, and blue,
There's always one door that is opened to you,
And that is the door to the house of prayer,
And you'll find God waiting
   to meet you there. . .
And the house of prayer is no farther away
Than the quiet spot where you kneel and pray.
For the heart is a temple when God is there
As we place ourselves in His loving care. . .
And He hears every prayer
   and answers each one
When we pray in His name,
   "Thy will be done."
And the burdens that seemed
   too heavy to bear
Are lifted away on the wings of prayer.

PRAYERS CAN'T BE ANSWERED
UNTIL THEY ARE PRAYED

Life without purpose is barren indeed,
There can't be a harvest unless you plant seed.
There can't be attainment unless there's a goal,
And man's but a robot unless there's a soul.
If we send no ships out, no ships will come in,
And unless there's a contest, nobody can win...
For games can't be won
  unless they are played,
And prayers can't be answered
  unless they are prayed...
So whatever is wrong with your life today,
You'll find a solution
  if you kneel down and pray
Not just for pleasure, enjoyment, and health,
Not just for honors, prestige, and wealth
But pray for a purpose
  to make life worth living,
And pray for the joy of unselfish giving...
For great is your gladness
  and rich your reward
When you make your life's purpose
  the choice of the Lord.

NOW I LAY ME DOWN TO SLEEP

I remember so well this prayer I said
Each night as my mother tucked me in bed,
And today this same prayer is still the best way
To sign off with God at the end of the day
And to ask Him your soul to safely keep
As you wearily close your tired eyes in sleep,
Feeling content that the Father above
Will hold you secure in His great arms of love.
And having His promise, that if ere you wake
His angels reach down, your sweet soul to take,
Is perfect assurance that, awake or asleep,
God is always right there to tenderly keep
All of His children ever safe in His care,
For God's here and He's there
   and He's everywhere.
So into His hands each night as I sleep
I commend my soul
   for the dear Lord to keep,
Knowing that if my soul should take flight
It will soar to the land
   where there is no night.

ETERNAL HOPE

A BEAUTIFUL BEGINNING FOR
PEACE ON EARTH

❧

Let us all remember
When our faith is running low
Christ is more than just a figure
Wrapped in an ethereal glow. . .
For He came and dwelled among us
And He knows our every need,
And He loves and understands us
And forgives each sinful deed.
He was crucified and buried
And rose again in glory,
And His promise of salvation
Makes the wondrous Christmas story
An abiding reassurance
That the little Christ child's birth
Was the beautiful beginning
Of God's plan for peace on earth.

BEHOLD, I BRING YOU
GOOD TIDINGS

Glad tidings herald the Christ child's birth—
Joy to the world and peace on earth,
Glory to God. . .let all men rejoice
And hearken once more to the angel's voice.
It matters not who or what you are—
All men can behold the Christmas star,
For the star that shone is shining still
In the hearts of men of peace and goodwill.
It offers the answers to every man's need,
Regardless of color or race or creed. . .
So joining together in brotherly love,
Let us worship again our Father above,
And forgetting our own little selfish desires,
May we seek what the star
  of Christmas inspires.

THE MAGIC OF LOVE

Love is like magic and it always will be,
For love still remains life's sweet mystery.
Love works in ways
	that are wondrous and strange,
And there's nothing in life
	that love cannot change.
Love can transform the most commonplace
Into beauty and splendor
	and sweetness and grace.
Love is unselfish, understanding, and kind,
For it sees with its heart
	and not with its mind.
Love gives and forgives;
	there is nothing too much
For love to heal with its magic touch.
Love is the language that every heart speaks,
For love is the one thing
	that every heart seeks...
And where there is love God, too, will abide
And bless the family residing inside.

THERE IS NO DEATH

There is no night without a dawning,
No winter without a spring,
And beyond death's dark horizon,
Our hearts once more will sing.
For those who leave us for a while
Have only gone away
Out of a restless, careworn world
Into a brighter day,
Where there will be no partings
And time is not counted by years,
Where there are no trials or troubles,
No worries, no cares, and no tears.

I DO NOT GO ALONE

If Death should beckon me
  with outstretched hand
And whisper softly of an unknown land,
I shall not be afraid to go,
For though the path I do not know,
I take Death's hand without fear,
For He who safely brought me here
Will also take me safely back,
And though in many things I lack,
He will not let me go alone
Into the valley that's unknown. . .
So I reach out and take Death's hand
And journey to the Promised Land.

FAITH IS A MIGHTY FORTRESS

❧

We look ahead through each changing year
With mixed emotions of hope and fear—
Unwilling to trust in the Father's will,
We count on our logic and shadow skill,
And in our arrogance and pride,
We are no longer satisfied.
Oh heavenly Father, grant again
A simple, childlike faith to men,
Forgotten color, race, and creed
And seeing only the heart's deep need.
For faith alone can save man's soul
And lead him to a higher goal,
For there's but one unfailing course—
We win by faith and not by force.

WITH GOD ALL THINGS
ARE POSSIBLE

Nothing is ever too hard to do
If your faith is strong
  and your purpose is true. . .
So never give up, and never stop—
Just journey on to the mountaintop!

SPIRITUAL LESSONS FROM PAIN

How little we know what God has in store
As daily He blesses our lives more and more.
I've lived many years
    and I've learned many things,
But today I have grown new spiritual wings...
For pain has a way of broadening our view
And bringing us closer in sympathy, too,
To those who are living in constant pain
And trying somehow to bravely sustain
The faith and endurance to keep on trying
When they almost welcome
    the peace of dying...
Without this experience
    I would have lived and died
Without fathoming the pain
    of Christ crucified,
For none of us knows what pain is all about
Until our spiritual wings start to sprout.
So thank You, God, for the gift You sent
To teach me that pain's heaven sent.

A MESSAGE OF CONSOLATION

On the wings of death and sorrow
God sends us new hope for tomorrow,
And in His mercy and His grace
He gives us strength to bravely face
The lonely days that stretch ahead
And to know our loved one is not dead
But only sleeping out of our sight,
And we'll meet in that land
   where there is no night.

SLOWING DOWN

My days are so crowded and my hours so few
And I can no longer work fast like I used to do.
But I know I must learn to be satisfied
That God has not completely denied
The joy of working—at a much slower pace—
For as long as He gives me a little place
To work with Him in His vineyard of love,
Just to know that He's
    helping me from above
Gives me strength to meet each day
As I travel along life's changing way.

A PART OF ME

Dear God, You are a part of me—
You're all I do and all I see;
You're what I say and what I do,
For all my life belongs to You.
You walk with me and talk with me,
For I am Yours eternally,
And when I stumble, slip, and fall
Because I'm weak and lost and small,
You help me up and take my hand
And lead me toward the Promised Land.
I cannot dwell apart from You—
You would not ask or want me to,
For You have room within Your heart
To make each child of Yours a part
Of You and all Your love and care
If we but come to You in prayer.

SOMEBODY CARES

Somebody cares and always will—
The world forgets, but God loves you still.
You cannot go beyond His love
No matter what you're guilty of,
For God forgives until the end,
He is your faithful, loyal friend.
And though you try to hide your face,
There is no shelter anyplace
That can escape His watchful eye,
For on the earth and in the sky
He's ever-present and always there
To take you in His tender care
And bind the wounds and mend the breaks
When all the world around forsakes.
Somebody cares and loves you still,
And God is the someone who always will.

BIRTHDAYS ARE A GIFT
FROM GOD

Where does time go in its endless flight?
Spring turns to fall and day to night,
And birthdays come and birthdays go,
And where they go we do not know...
But God, who planned our life on earth
And gave our minds and bodies birth,
And then enclosed a living soul
With heaven as the spirit's goal,
Has given man the gift of choice
To follow that small inner voice
That speaks to us from year to year,
Reminding us we've naught to fear...
So fill each day with happy things,
And may your burdens all take wing
And fly away and leave behind
Great joy of heart and peace of mind...
For birthdays are the gateway to
An endless life of joy for you
If you but pray from day to day
That He will show you the truth and the way.

REMEMBRANCE ROAD

There's a road I call remembrance
   where I walk each day with you.
It's a pleasant, happy road, my dear,
   all filled with memories true.
Today it lead me through a spot
   where I can dream awhile,
And in its tranquil peacefulness
   I touch your hand and smile.
There are hills and fields and budding trees
   and stillness that's so sweet
That it seems that this must be the place
   where God and humans meet.
I hope we can go back again
   and golden hours, renew,
And God go with you always, dear,
   until the day we do.

GLORY TO GOD

"Glory to God in the highest, and on
  earth peace, goodwill toward men."
May the angels' song of long ago
  ring in our hearts again
And bring a new awareness
  that the fate of every nation
Is sealed securely in the hand
  of the Maker of creation. . .
For man, with all his knowledge,
  his wisdom, and his skill,
Is powerless to go beyond
  the holy Father's will. . .
And when we fully recognize
  the helplessness of man
And seek our Father's guidance
  in our every thought and plan,
Then only can we build a world
  of faith and hope and love,
And only then can man achieve
  the life he's dreaming of.

INDEX